Published by: Legna Studio
ISBN: 979-8-218-40729-2
Cover Design: Angel Garza
Illustrations: Angel Garza
Text: Angel Garza
First Edition: 2024

100% designed, illustrated and printed in the United States of America

For permissions requests or inquiries, please contact:
Legna Studio | legnastudioco@gmail.com | legna-studio.square.site

Trademark and Image Protection:
The logo, illustrations, and all images contained within this coloring book are protected by copyright law. Unauthorized use, reproduction, or distribution of these materials is strictly prohibited and may result in legal action.

Use of Public Locations:
Some illustrations within this coloring book may depict public locations such as state parks and landmarks. While every effort has been made to accurately represent these locations, the publisher and author do not claim ownership of these sites. Their inclusion is for artistic and educational purposes only.

Disclaimer:
The publisher and author have made every effort to ensure the accuracy of the information herein. However, due to the ever-changing nature of historical and geographical data, no warranty or representation, express or implied, is made as to the completeness, accuracy, or reliability of the content. The publisher and author shall not be liable for any loss, damage, or injury arising from the use of this coloring book or the information contained herein. Readers

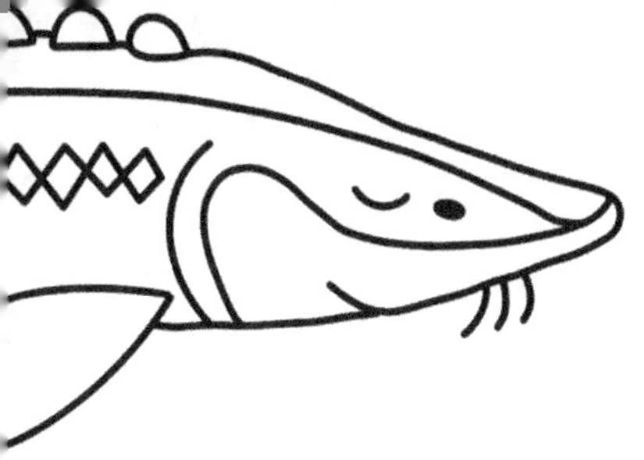

Welcome to the Gorge: Less Portlandia, More Fun!

Alright listen up, explorers and color enthusiasts! Forget the fuss and feathers of Portland, we're trading city streets for the real star of the show: The Columbia River Gorge! This place is bursting with adventure - think epic waterfalls, adorable towns like something out of a storybook, and a secret or two hidden around every bend (but maybe stick to the trails, explorers - some things are best left mysterious, like your grandpa's hat collection).

Before We Crayon Our Way to Fun:
Let's sprinkle in a bit of history. Long before anyone got lost with a bad case of the "wilderness wanders" (looking at you, Lewis and Clark!), this land belonged to many incredible Native American tribes. The Chinook, Multnomah, and Wasco people lived here in harmony with nature, fishing the rivers and respecting the mighty salmon - the Beyoncés of the fish world!

Back to the Future:
Dial the flux capacitor in your DeLorean forward a few centuries when pioneers showed up, building towns that are now charming stops on our adventure. Our first stop, Troutdale, used to be called Sandy - way less exciting, like a bowl of plain oatmeal (unless you're a superfan of beige, which is totally okay!). Then there's Cascade Locks, built to help boats navigate the tricky rapids, like a highway for fancy steamboats that chugged up and down the river (think of them as the Uber of the 1800s, but without the app!).

Now Let's Get Colorful!
Alright, enough history for now! Grab your crayons, markers, or whatever fancy doodling tools you have. We've got majestic waterfalls to color, forests so green they'd make a leprechaun jealous, and hidden trails waiting to be explored (with a map, of course - we don't want any mini Lewis and Clarks getting lost!).

This coloring book is your chance to turn the Gorge into your own masterpiece. So ditch the boring beige and unleash your inner artist! Because in the Gorge, the only thing wilder than the scenery is your imagination (and maybe your grandpa's hat collection, but that's a story for another time).

Explore & Color Scavenger Hunt

Time Travel: First stop, the Troutdale Historical Society's Barn Exhibit Hall! Color that barn red and explore all the cool stuff inside. Head next door to the Fred E. Harlow House Museum and imagine what life was like a bazillion years ago. Can you spot any old-timey furniture or clothes?

Wildlife Spotting: Keep your peepers peeled for critters as we drive along! Color a bluebird at Glenn Otto Park, and if you see a real one, give it a big thumbs-up!

Waterfall Wonder: Get ready to be wowed by Multnomah Falls! Use all the blues and greens in your crayon box to make it look super spectacular. And count those switchbacks if you can tear your eyes away from the beauty!

Bridge of the Gods: This bridge is like something out of a fairy tale! Color it all bright and cheery with reds and oranges, and imagine the magical stories it holds.

Vista Point View: Crown Point Vista House has views that'll make your heart sing! Splash those colors onto your paper and make it as beautiful as the real thing.

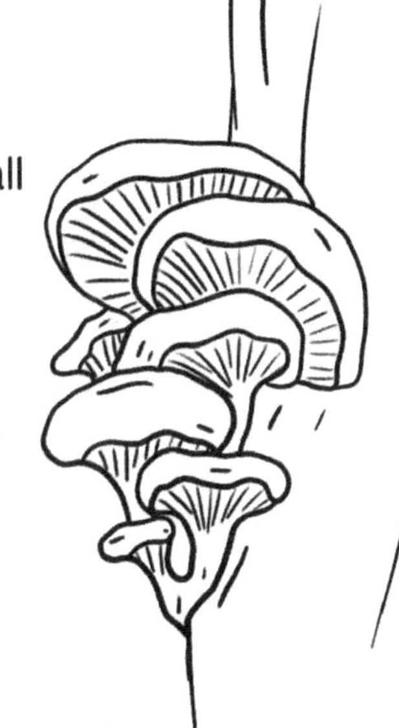

Turn on the Lights: Bonneville Dam is a superhero of electricity! Color those walls and fish ladders while learning about the fishy friends who call it home.

Cascade Locks: This town is like something from a storybook! Color the stern-wheeler in the brightest colors you can find, and let your imagination run wild.

Nature's Canvas: Hike to Latourell Falls and let nature's beauty fill your heart with joy. Then, use your crayons to capture it on paper with lots of greens and sparkles!

Treasure Chest: Phew, we made it! Find the hidden picnic area at Ainsworth State Park and have a snack. Color those tables and trees like you're having the best picnic ever!

And hey, if you're feeling extra adventurous, collect a leaf from each spot and make a super special keepsake to remember our awesome adventure together!

Just remember, pals: Be kind to the environment, stay safe, and let your imagination soar higher than a kite in a windstorm!

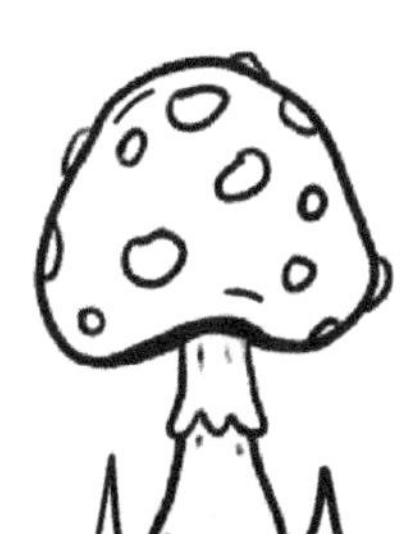

Gorge-ous Troutdale

Downtown Troutdale: Come take a stroll through the charming streets of Downtown Troutdale and delve into its fascinating history. Did you know that the town was originally named Sandy, after the nearby Sandy River? It wasn't until 1873 that it earned its current name, Troutdale, in honor of Captain John Harlow, a local pioneer who ran a salmon-trading post. Today, the town maintains its nostalgic appeal with historic buildings and quaint shops, serving as the perfect launching point for your adventure into the Columbia River Gorge. But first, indulge in some delectable local bites to fuel your exploration!

exploretroutdale.com

Barn Exhibit Hall: Intrigued by the stories of the Wild West? Take a step back in time at the Troutdale Historical Society's Barn Exhibit Hall and immerse yourself in the world of pioneers and trailblazers. Did you know that the construction of the Historic Columbia River Highway, often dubbed the "King of Roads," was a remarkable engineering feat of its era? Explore the exhibits showcasing antique tools, and artifacts that narrate the tale of early settlement and the evolution of this iconic highway. Don't forget to visit the Rail Depot and the Harlow House, where more treasures from Troutdale's past await discovery. Just a heads up, some of the delicate exhibits at the Harlow House may not be suitable for younger history enthusiasts. So, let curiosity guide you as you uncover the layers of Troutdale's heritage! Join the Troutdale Historical Society today and step into the shoes of those who shaped local history. Volunteers are always welcome to help preserve the history of this wonderful town!

troutdalehistory.org | Admission: $5; Free for Members & Multnomah County Residents | Free Parking

Glenn Otto Park: Trade city noise for the soothing whispers of the Sandy River at Glenn Otto Park. Lush greenery paints the scene, creating a haven of tranquility. This park pays homage to a local champion who fought to preserve the Columbia River Gorge's natural beauty. Escape the crowds and find serenity in this idyllic oasis. Feeling the heat? Take a refreshing dip in the cool waters of the Sandy River, or grab an inner tube and float along its gentle current.
Pro Tip: Be sure to check current water conditions and safety information before tubing.

troutdaleoregon.gov | Admission: Free | Free Parking

Sandy River Delta Park: Embrace the wild beauty of Sandy River Delta Park (also known as 1,000 Acres). This expansive park offers 1,400 acres for outdoor enthusiasts to explore. Hike, bike, or horseback ride along scenic trails, or cool off with a swim in the Sandy or Columbia River. Keep your eyes peeled – over 200 bird species call this park home! With wide-open spaces and endless trails, it's like having your own private nature preserve.

fs.usda.gov | Admission: Free | $5 per day parking; Free with NW Forest Pass, "Every Kid Outdoors", "America the Beautiful" or Golden Age/Access

Maya Lin Confluence Bird Blind: Calling all bird enthusiasts! Tucked away in Sandy River Delta Park is the Maya Lin Confluence Bird Blind, designed by the famed artist behind the Vietnam Veterans Memorial. This unique structure offers a prime spot for birdwatching,putting you face-to-face with the feathered residents of the area. Relax in the comfortable viewing area and enjoy the symphony of bird calls without needing binoculars or bug spray. It's a tranquil escape perfect for observing nature up close.

fs.usda.gov | Admission: Free | $5 per day parking; Free with NW Forest Pass, "Every Kid Outdoors", "America the Beautiful" or Golden Age/Access

Oxbow Regional Park: Carve out an escape at Oxbow Regional Park, a 1,000-acre playground nestled within the Columbia River Gorge. The Sandy River takes center stage, snaking through the park like a shimmering emerald ribbon. Hike or bike along scenic trails, with options for all levels. Feeling adventurous? Kayak or paddleboard on the calm waters, or cast a line and try your luck fishing.

History buffs will appreciate the park's ancient forest, boasting trees hundreds of years old. Keep your eyes peeled for wildlife – you might spot deer, beavers, or even elusive black bears. After a day of exploration, unwind by the riverbank or have a picnic at one of the designated areas. The park offers year-round camping, making it the perfect base for exploring the Columbia River Gorge.

oregonmetro.gov | Admission: Free | $5 per Car Parking or $7 per Bus; Free with Annual Parking Pass

Dodge Park: Dodge Park beckons nature lovers seeking tranquility along the banks of the Sandy River. Towering trees and the gentle murmur of flowing water create a serene atmosphere, perfect for unwinding and reconnecting with the outdoors. Enjoy a picnic by the river, explore scenic trails, or simply soak up the peaceful ambiance. Dodge Park offers a haven for relaxation and rejuvenation.

Adventurer's Alert: The park map marks a "secret beach" – a hidden gem for those seeking adventure. Remember, the map may not be perfectly scaled, so explore cautiously if you choose to venture off the beaten path. With a little planning and a love for nature, Dodge Park promises a refreshing escape for everyone.

portland.gov | Admission: Free | Free Parking

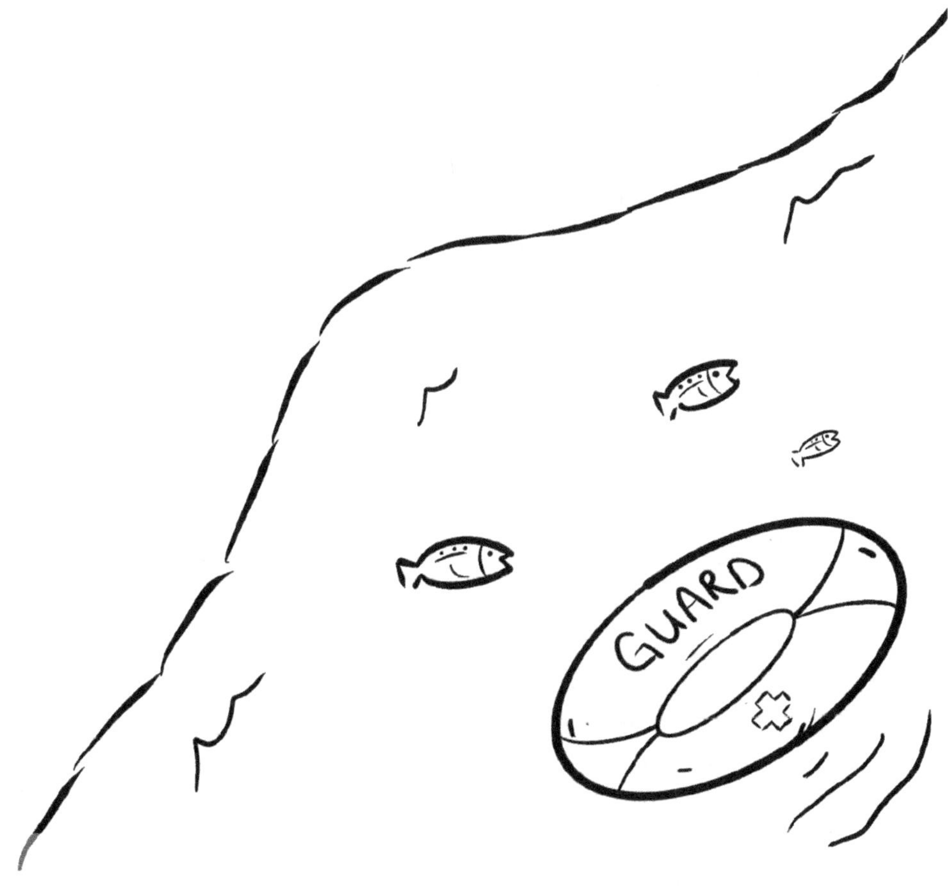

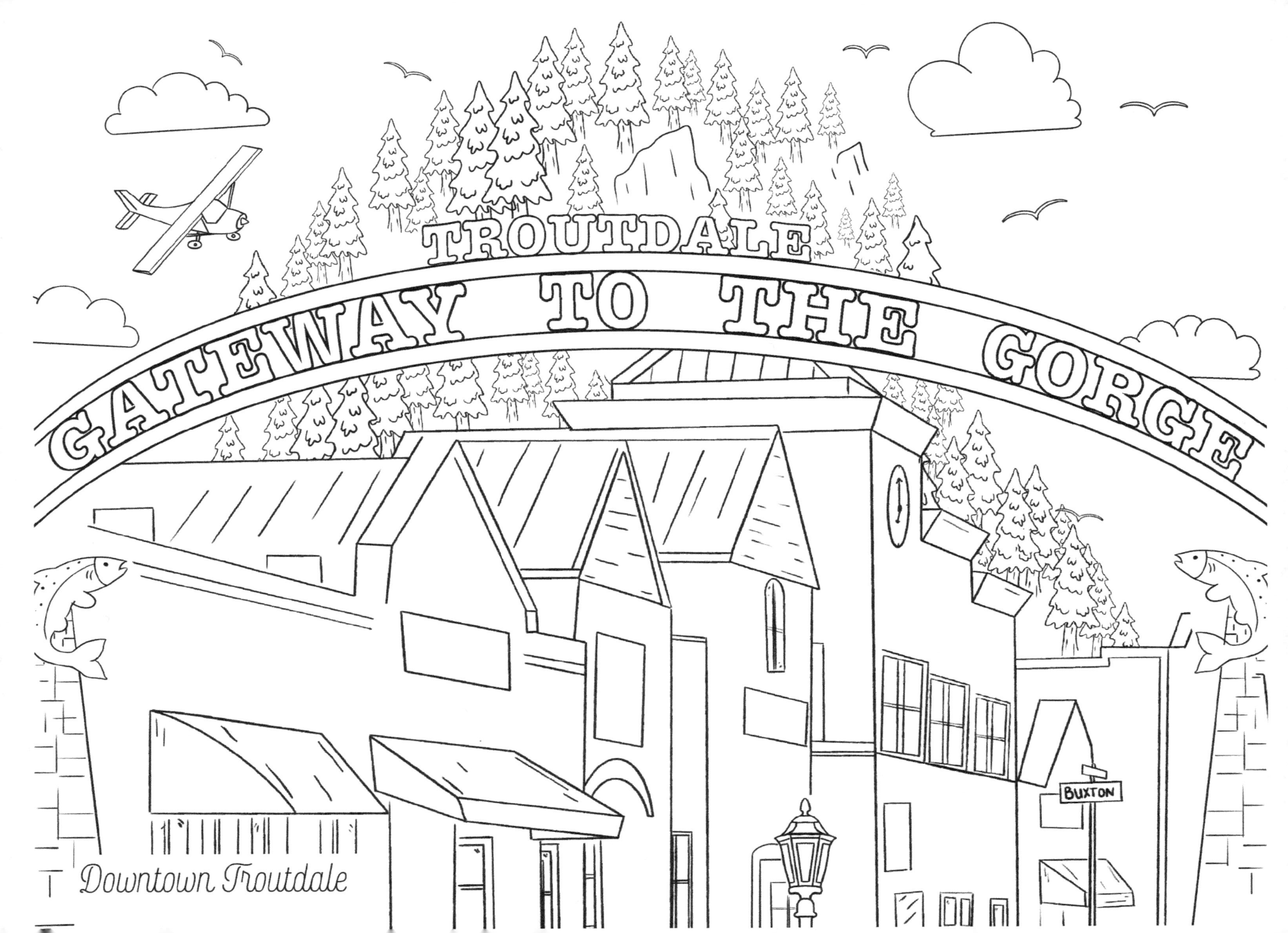

TROUTDALE
GATEWAY TO THE GORGE
BUXTON
Downtown Troutdale

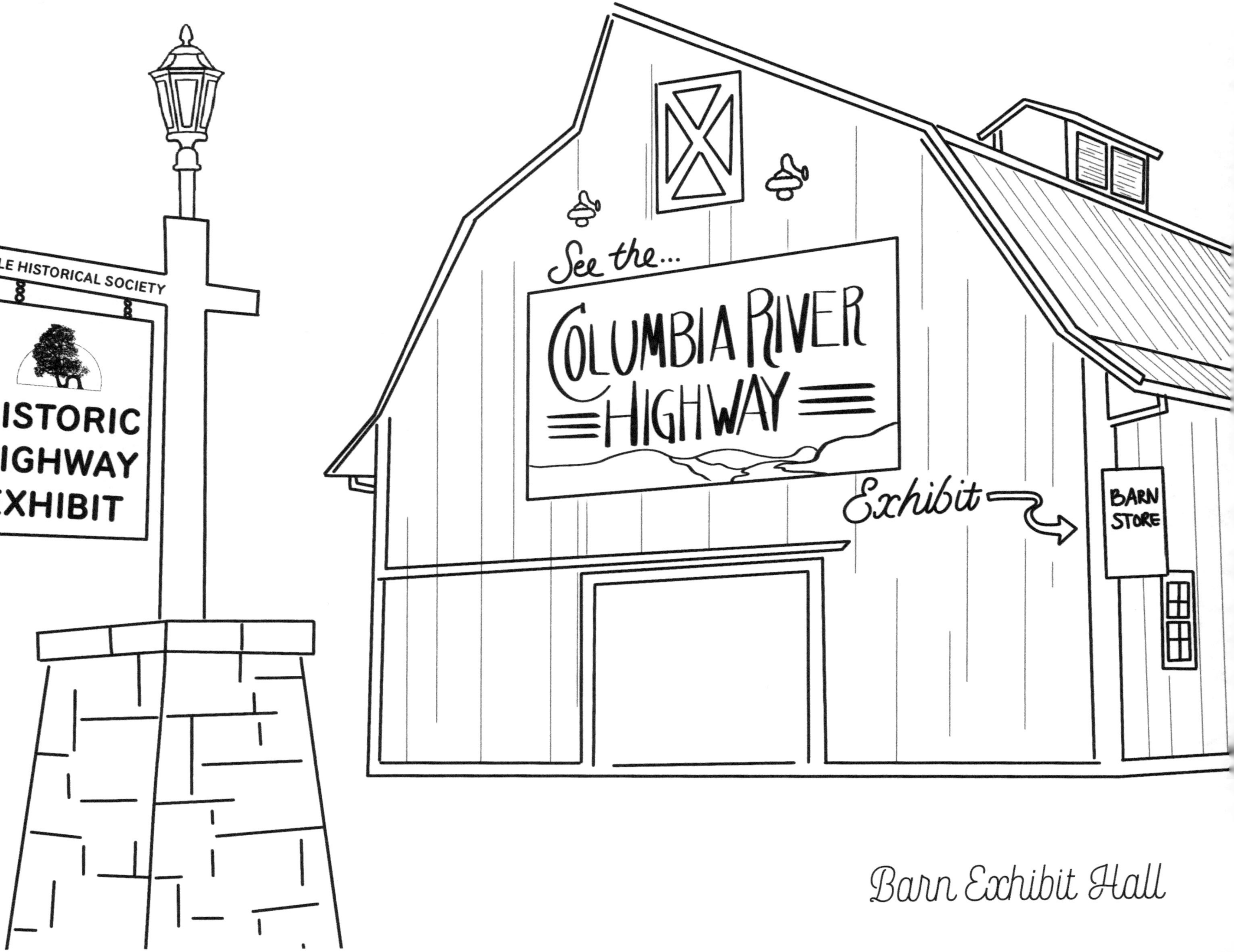

Barn Exhibit Hall

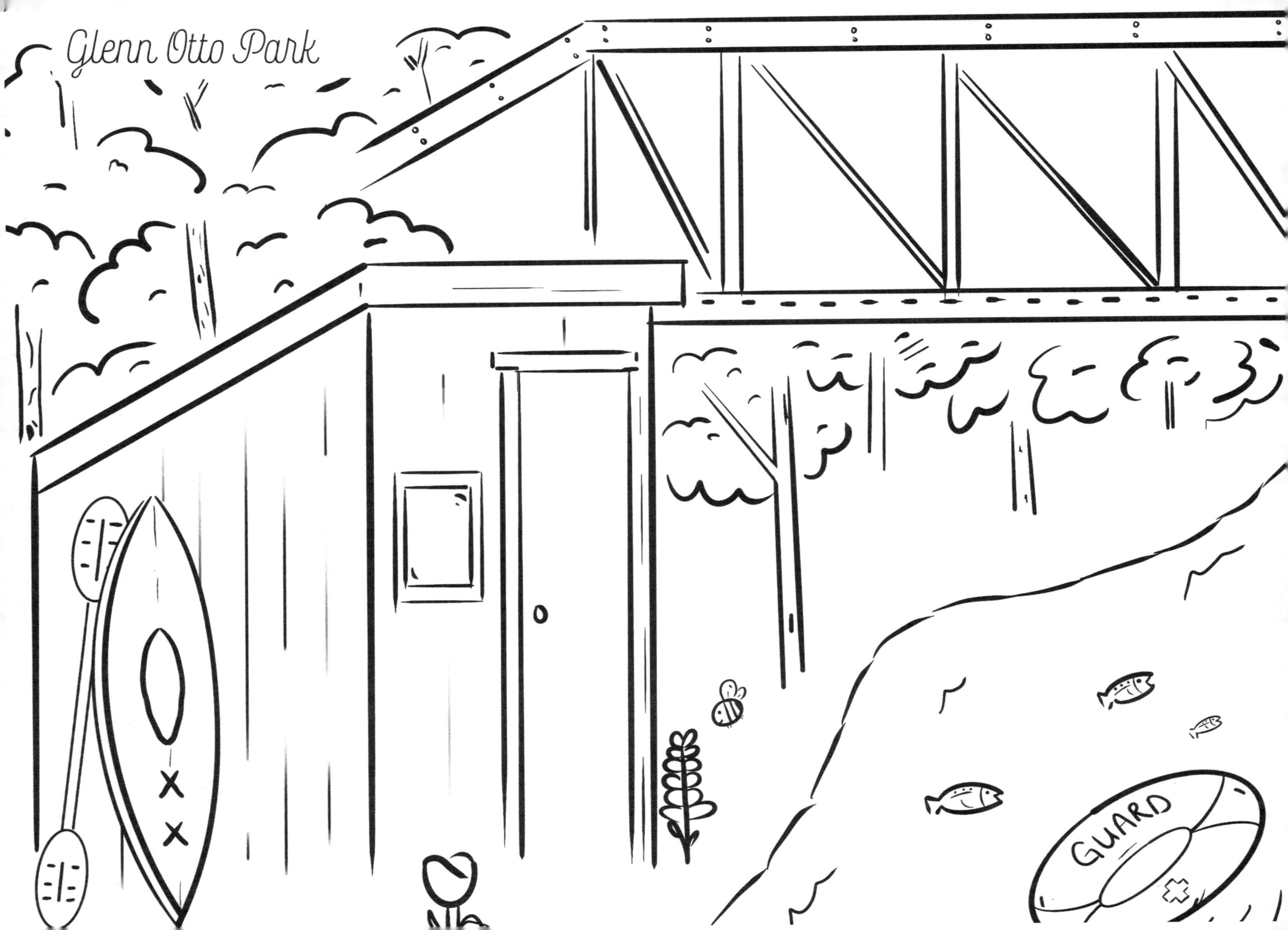

Glenn Otto Park
GUARD

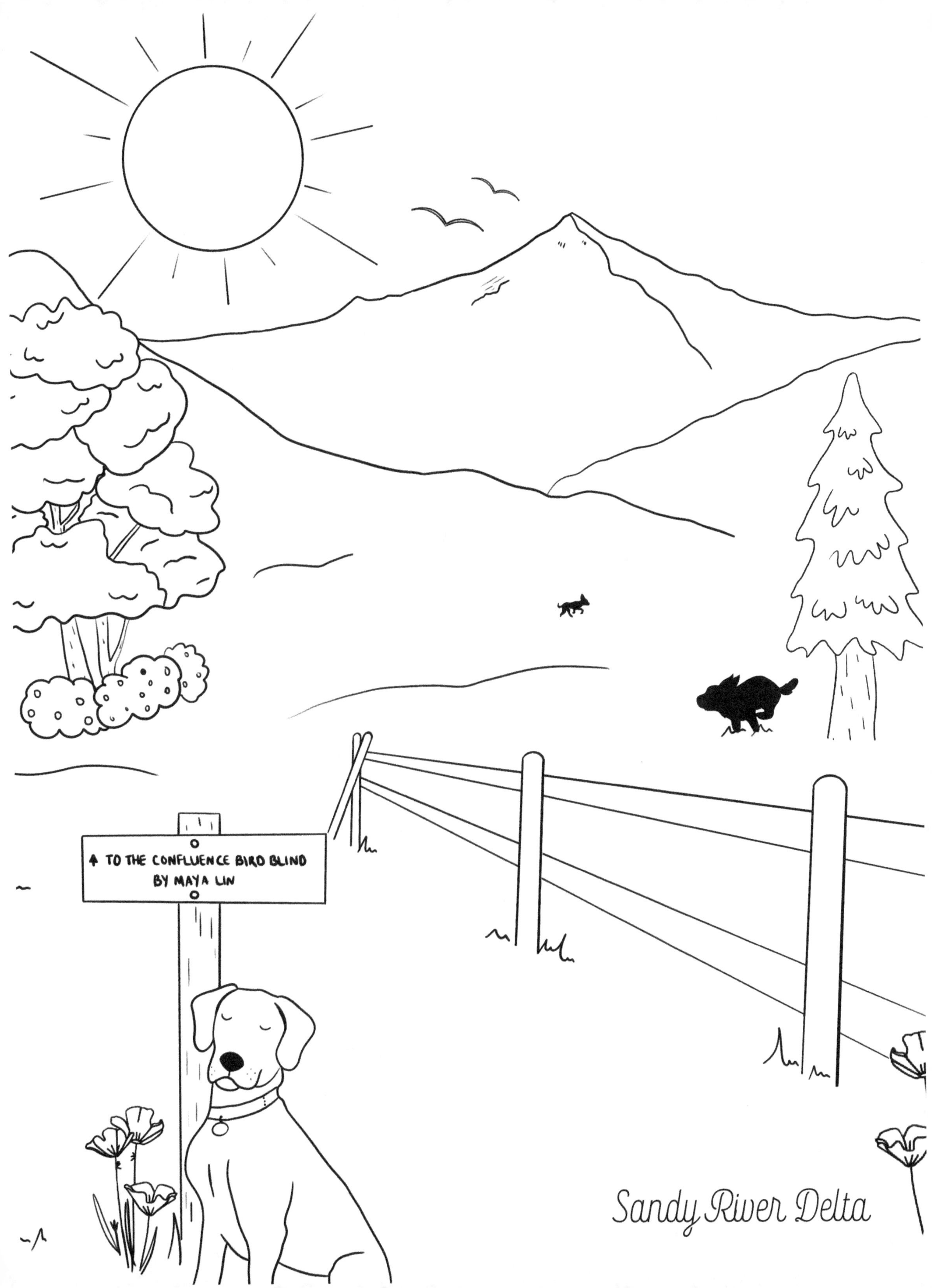

4 TO THE CONFLUENCE BIRD BLIND
BY MAYA LIN
Sandy River Delta

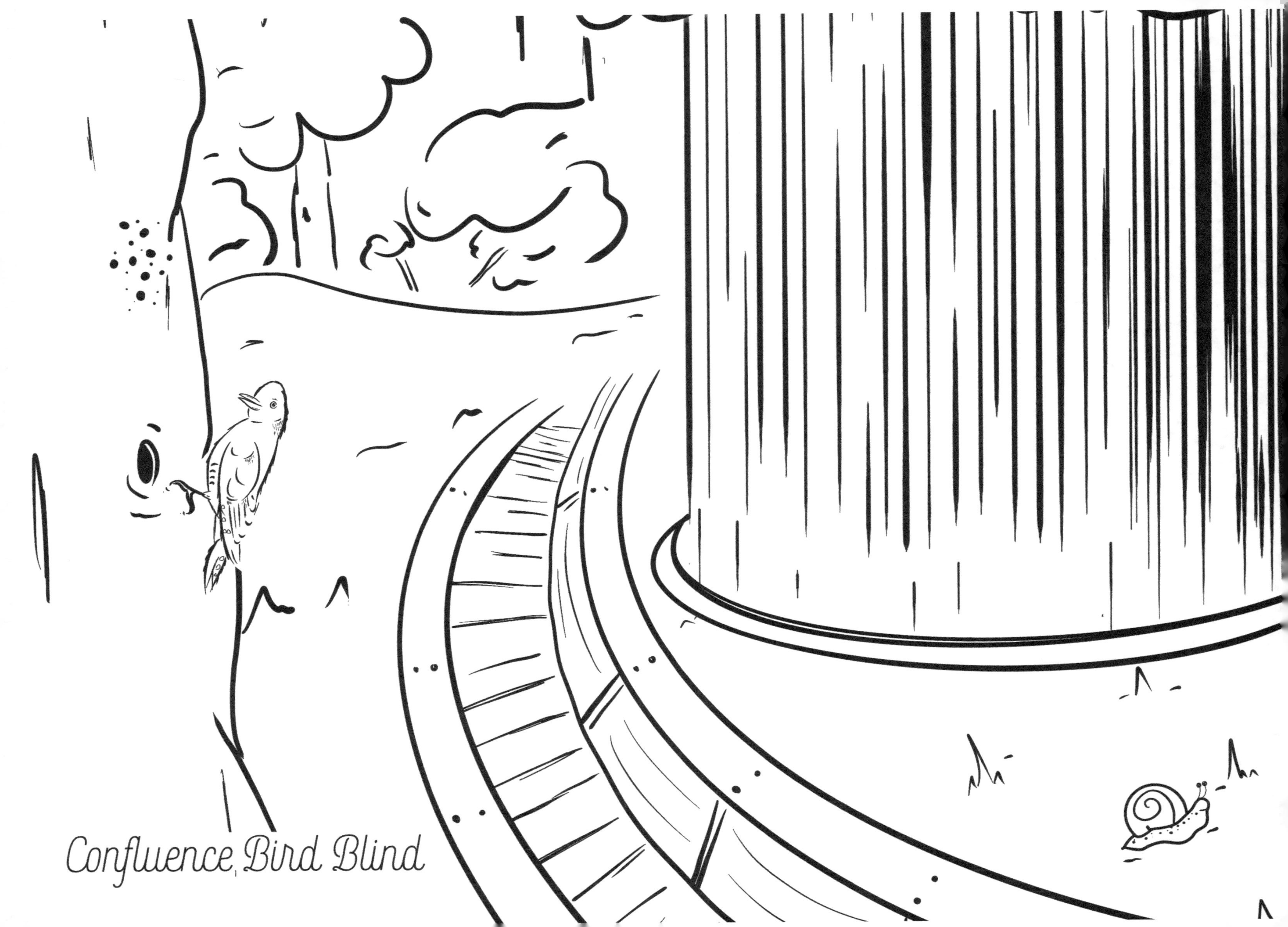

Confluence Bird Blind

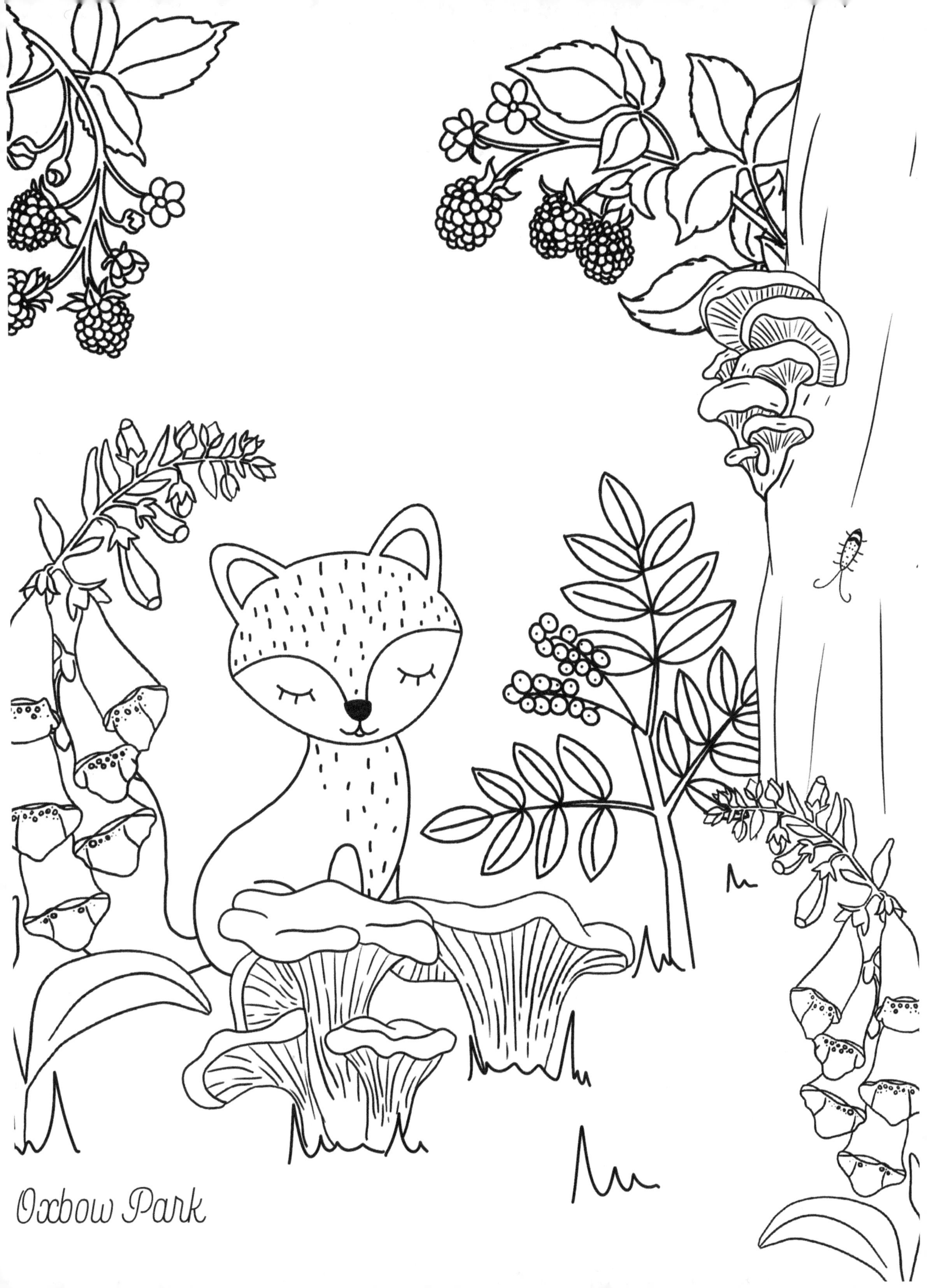
Oxbow Park

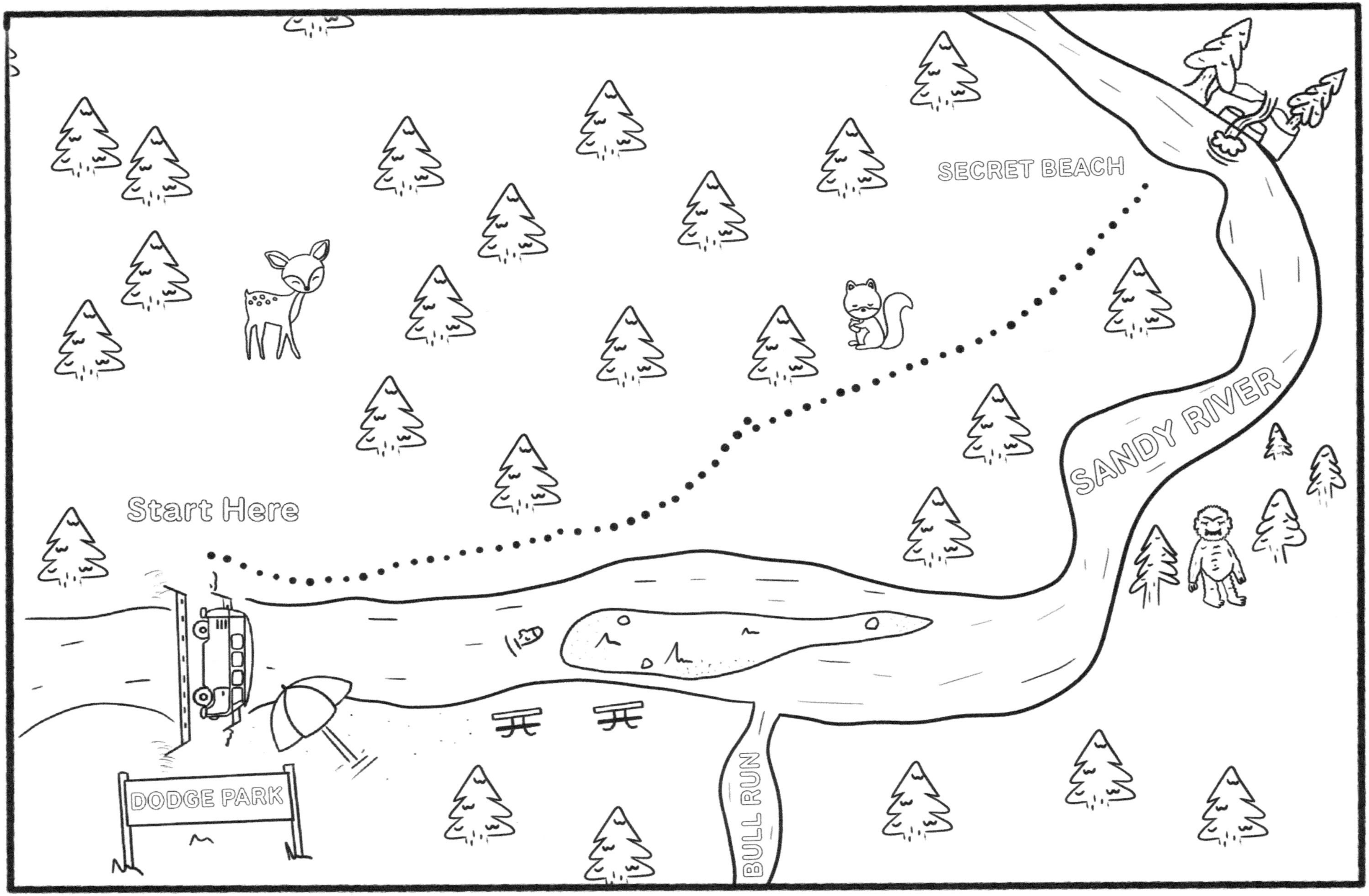

Secret Beach at Dodge Park

* map is not to scale

Gorge-ous Historic Highway

Corbett Country Market: Nestled in the heart of the Columbia River Gorge, Corbett Country Mart offers more than just gas and snacks. This historic market, established decades ago, is a local treasure brimming with charm. Originally a small general store, it's become a beloved community hub for locals and travelers. Friendly faces greet you as you step inside, and the atmosphere is steeped in nostalgia. Browse for unique finds and local treats, or simply soak up the historic ambiance. Corbett Country Mart isn't just a pit stop – it's a delightful slice of Gorge life.

corbettcountrymarket.com

Portland Women's Forum: No journey through the Gorge would be complete without a visit to Portland Women's Forum, offering a breathtaking vista of the historic landmark nestled in the embrace of the Columbia River Gorge. This picturesque sight not only captivates globetrotters from far and wide but also inspired the pioneers behind the Historic Columbia River Highway. Imagine, in 1918, they crafted the very first road linking Portland and The Dalles, all inspired by this panoramic spectacle. And guess what? This little park owes its existence to none other than the Portland Women's Forum, a group of trailblazers dedicated to preserving Mother Nature's finest. They even generously gifted this land to the state! Swing by and experience firsthand why this spot has become a photography hotspot, capturing the essence of Vista House. Psst, rumor has it you might just catch a glimpse of this majestic view on the cover of your coloring book!

stateparks.oregon.gov | Admission: Free | Free Parking

Crown Point Vista House: Perched majestically atop Crown Point, Vista House reigns supreme as the crown jewel of the Columbia River Gorge. Since 1918, this octagonal wonder, designed by architect Edgar M. Lazarus, has mesmerized visitors with its marble floors, stained glass windows, and tributes to Oregon Trail pioneers. Visit between 6 a.m. and 9 p.m. to explore the museum and snag some goodies from the gift shop, but keep an eye on the wind – Vista House closes at 50 mph gusts! And while you're there, kick off your waterfall quest with a visit to Multnomah Falls because, let's be real, who can resist a cascade or two? Feeling extra spirited? Join the Friends of Vista House crew and be part of preserving Gorge history – they're the real MVPs!

vistahouse.com | Admission: Free | Free Parking

Sherrard Point: Sherrard Point, perched atop Larch Mountain, is a must-visit for hikers and nature lovers. This scenic overlook offers panoramic views of the Columbia River Gorge, with a majestic Mount Hood dominating the horizon. Be prepared for potentially strong winds at the summit!
The trail to Sherrard Point is a moderately challenging 3.7 miles out and back. Keep your eyes peeled for wildlife like mountain goats, and appreciate the diverse alpine plants clinging to the mountainside. Pack a picnic and enjoy the breathtaking views from the top.

fs.usda.gov | Admission: Free | Free Parking

Latourell Falls: Latourell Falls, a cascading wonder at 224 feet, is a must-see for any Columbia River Gorge visitor. Its easy accessibility makes it a favorite for families and nature enthusiasts of all levels. Witness the ethereal beauty of the falls and feel the refreshing spray as the water tumbles down. Breathe in the crisp air and listen to the calming sounds of the rushing water.
Insider Tip: Explore the short trail leading to the base of the falls for a closer look. Feeling more adventurous? Hike the Latourell Falls Loop Trail for stunning views and a deeper immersion into the surrounding beauty. Latourell Falls offers a scenic escape and a chance to reconnect with nature's grandeur.

stateparks.oregon.gov | Admission: Free | Free Parking

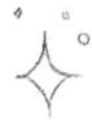

Multnomah Falls: Get swept away by the captivating Multnomah Falls, where nature's drama meets ancient legend. It's the kind of place that'll make you forget to Instagram for a minute and just soak it all in. It's like nature's own version of a mic drop.

According to the creation story of the Multnomah tribe, this iconic waterfall sprung forth from an act of extraordinary bravery. Picture this: a young woman, facing a plague threatening her village, boldly flings herself from the cliff to appease the Great Spirit and creates a magnificent waterfall. Now, as you stand in awe before the majestic cascade, reaching a mind blowing 620 feet, you can't help but feel the weight of this timeless tale echoing in the thundering waters. And hey, if you're up for some adventure, don't miss the nearby trails that weave through the lush forest, offering glimpses of hidden waterfalls and scenic overlooks. So lace up those hiking boots and let the spirit of Multnomah Falls guide you on an unforgettable journey through the wonders of the Columbia River Gorge.

stateparks.oregon.gov | Admission: Free | Free Parking

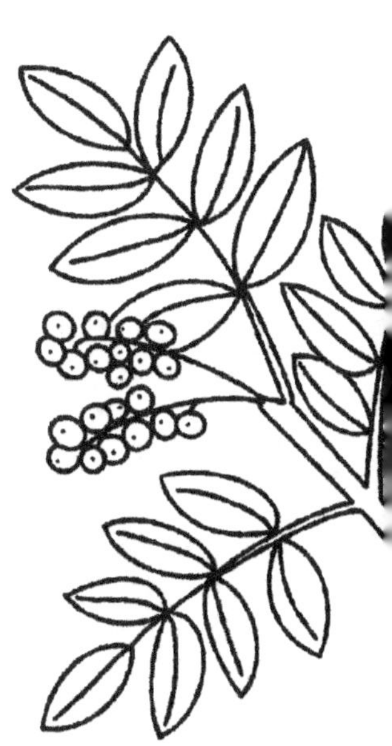

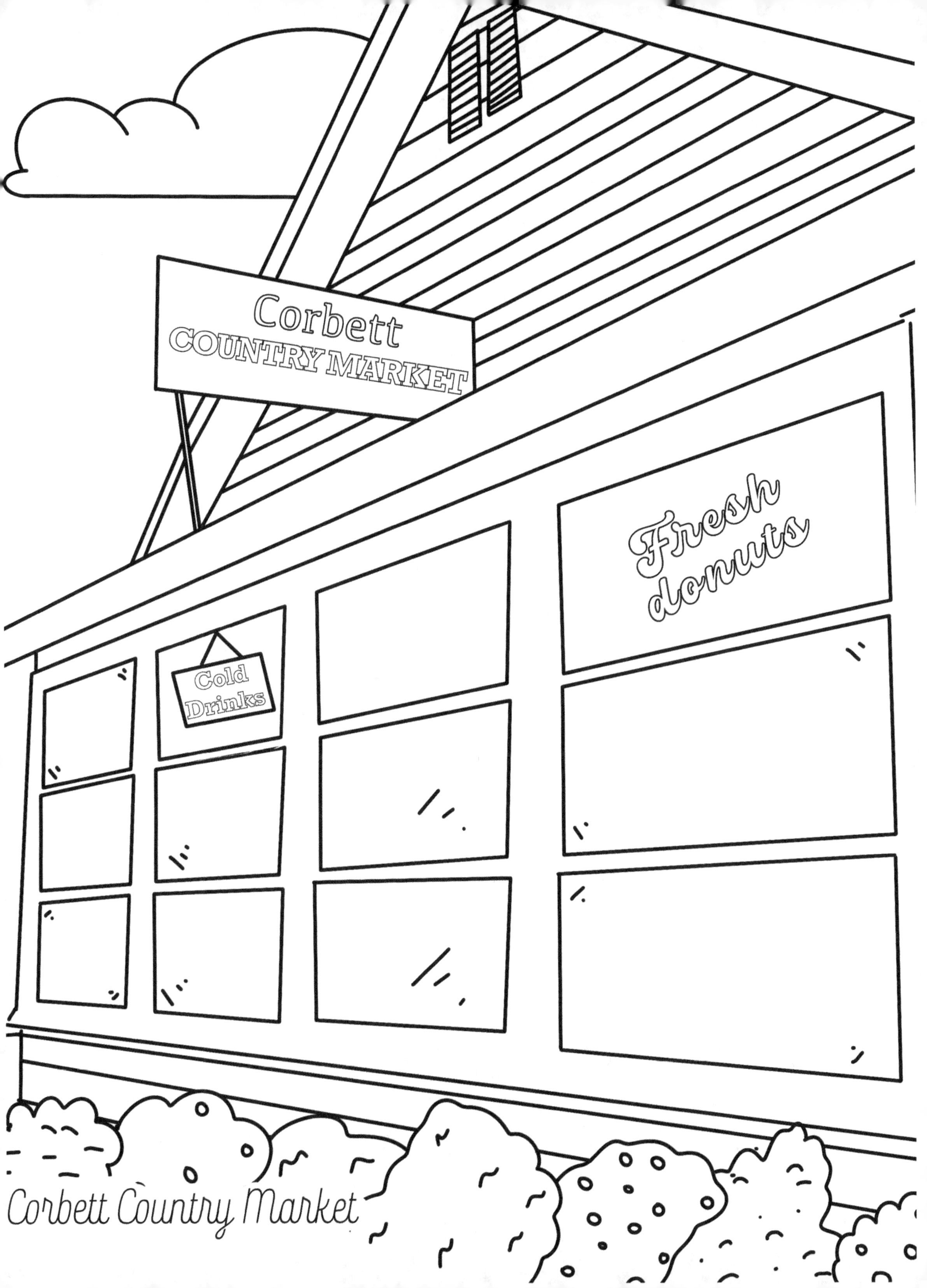

Corbett
COUNTRY MARKET
Fresh donuts
Cold Drinks
Corbett Country Market

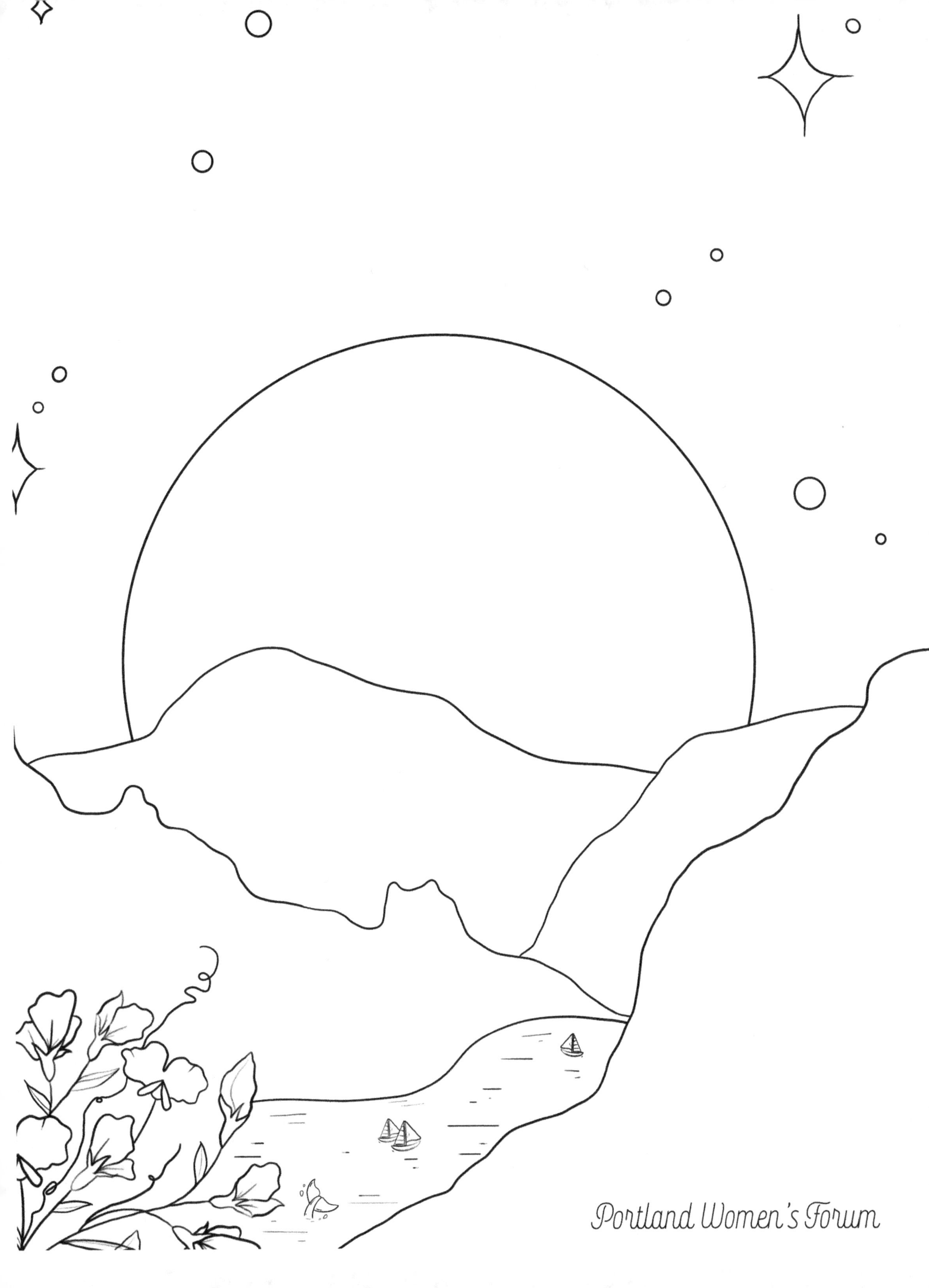
Portland Women's Forum

Crown Point Vista House

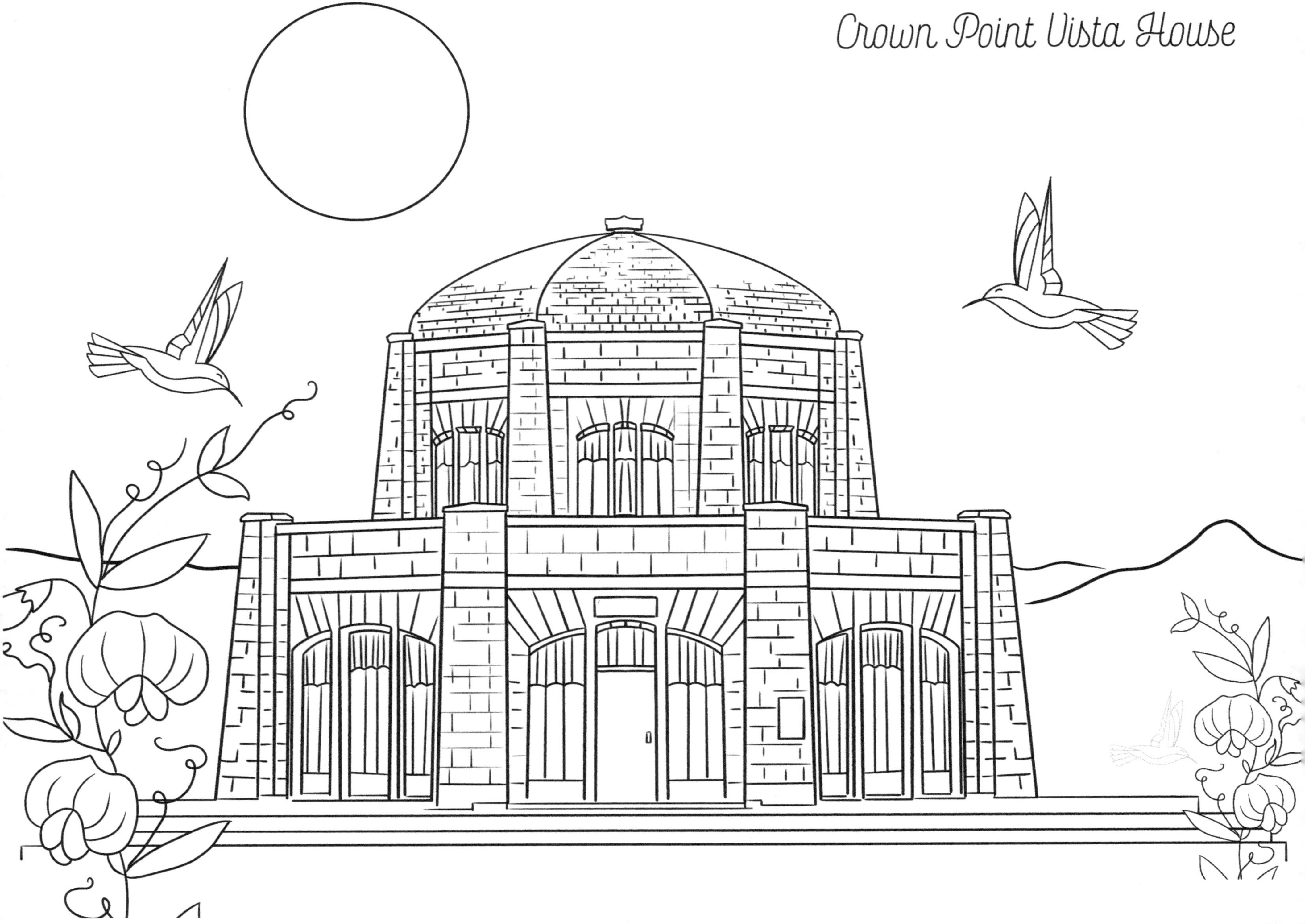

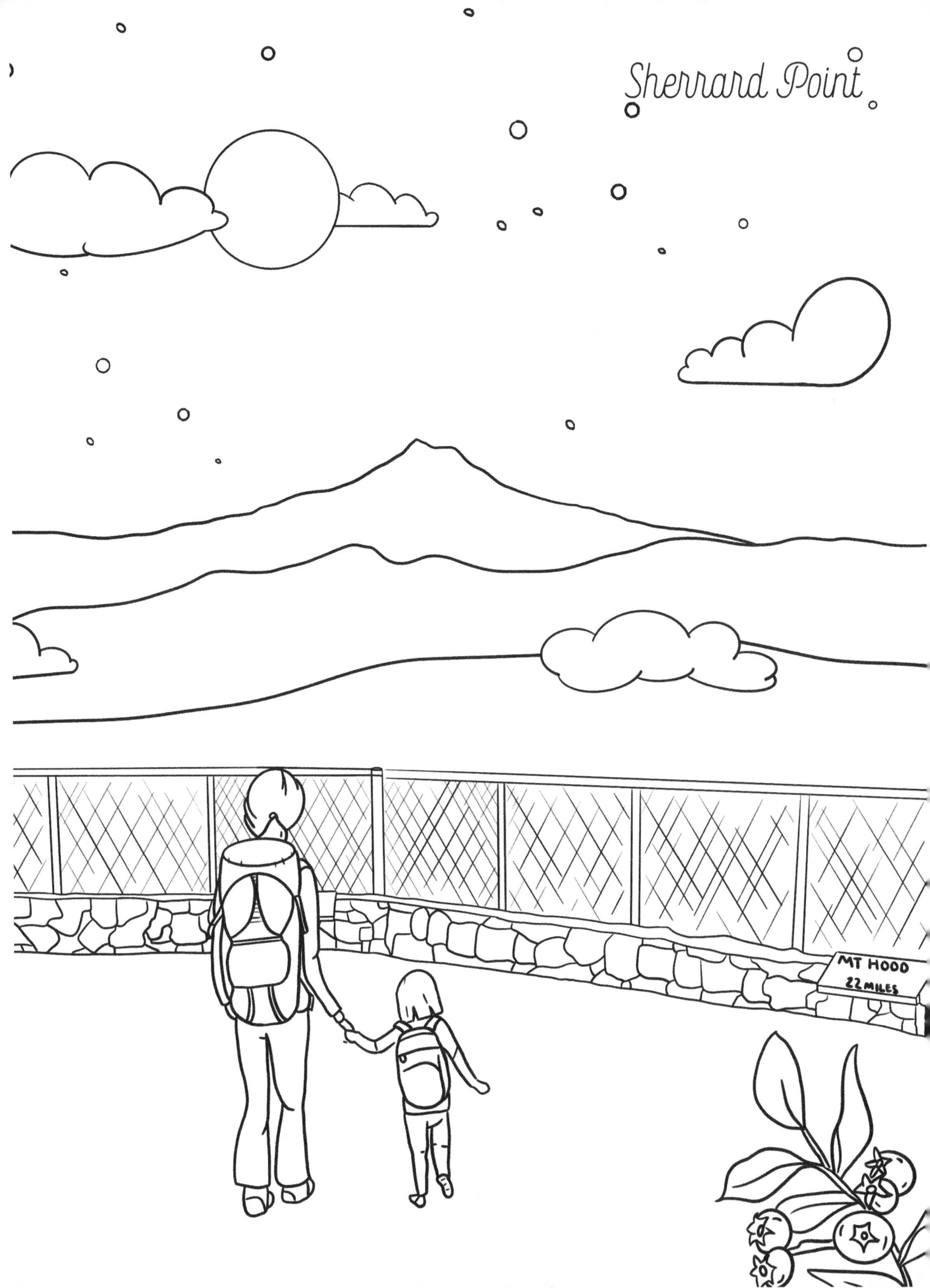

Sherrard Point
MT HOOD
22 MILES

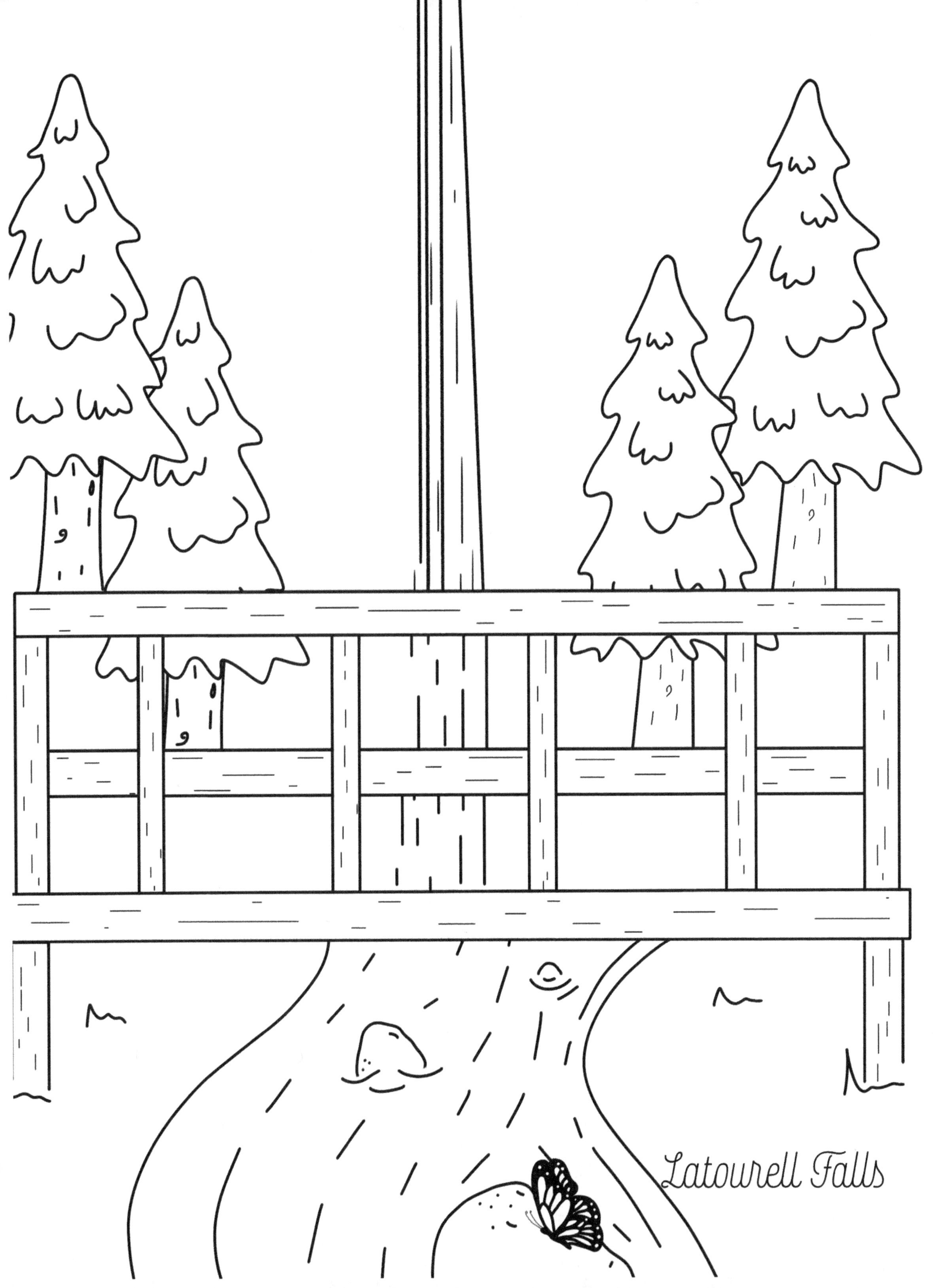

Latourell Falls

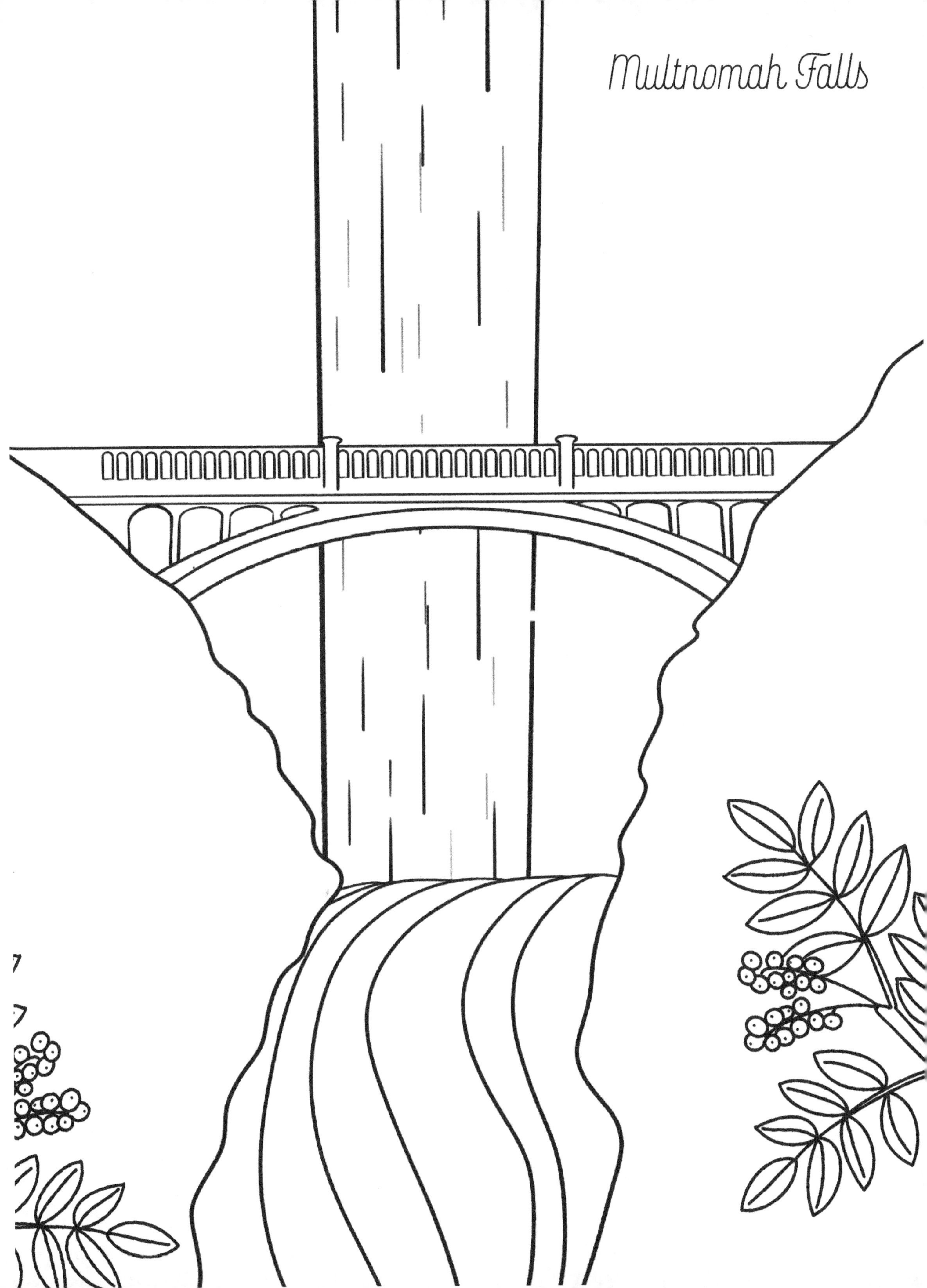

Multnomah Falls

Gorge-ous Cascade Locks

Ainsworth State Park: Beyond its scenic beauty, this park boasts a rich history, named after pioneer George J. Ainsworth. Hike through verdant forests, explore scenic trails, or simply relax by the water's edge. Whether you crave adventure or peaceful reflection, Ainsworth State Park offers something for everyone. With a seasonal campground and easy access to nearby waterfalls, this park is your gateway to unforgettable experiences in the Gorge.

stateparks.oregon.gov | Admission: Free | Free Parking

Bonneville Fish Hatchery: Established in 1909, this historic facility plays a crucial role in salmon and steelhead restoration efforts in the Columbia River Gorge. Witness the fascinating lifecycle of these fish through informative exhibits. A true crowd-pleaser is Herman the Sturgeon, a resident since the 1940s and one of the oldest and largest freshwater fish in North America! Feed the smaller fish, learn about conservation efforts, and be amazed by Herman's size – Bonneville Fish Hatchery offers a fun and educational experience for the whole family.

myodfw.com | Admission: Free | Free Parking

Bonneville Dam: Witness the awe-inspiring Bonneville Dam, a marvel of engineering completed in 1938. This iconic structure not only harnesses the Columbia River's power for clean, renewable energy but also plays a vital role in fish migration. Observe salmon surging through the fish ladders during their annual upstream journey (late spring to early summer). Whether you're a history enthusiast, nature lover, or simply seeking an unforgettable experience, Bonneville Dam offers something for everyone.

travelportland.com | Admission: Free | Free Parking

Bridge of the Gods: Legend whispers across the Columbia River Gorge as you traverse the Bridge of the Gods, a steel marvel connecting Oregon and Washington. Breathtaking vistas unfold beneath you, echoing the journeys of countless travelers before you. This iconic bridge isn't just a crossing; it's a symbol of unity and human ingenuity, standing proud against nature's grandeur. Explore the Cascade Locks Historical Museum and delve into the region's rich heritage, perhaps catching a glimpse of a familiar scene from the movie "Wild." Consider joining their efforts to preserve this history – every contribution helps! Refuel at local eateries and soak in the town's rustic charm before continuing your adventure.

portofcascadelocks.org | Toll: Starts at $3 per Vehicle

Columbia River Sternwheeler: Relive the grandeur of river travel aboard the Columbia River Sternwheeler, an authentic triple-decker paddle wheeler built in 1983. Cruise along the mighty Columbia, taking in 360-degree views of towering cliffs, lush forests, and cascading waterfalls. Knowledgeable guides narrate the rich history and natural wonders of the Gorge. Capture stunning photos and create lasting memories on this unique adventure. Perfect for history buffs, nature lovers, and anyone seeking a charming escape.

sternwheeler.com | See website for current cruise prices

Brigham Fish Market: Family tradition meets local flavor at Brigham Fish Market in Cascade Locks. Sisters Terrie Brigham and Kim Brigham-Campbell, members of the Confederated Tribes of the Umatilla Indian Reservation, honor generations of fishing heritage.They offer the freshest wild-caught fish straight from the Columbia River, including seasonal sturgeon, salmon, and steelhead. Support local traditions and savor the taste of the Gorge at Brigham Fish Market!

brighamfish.com

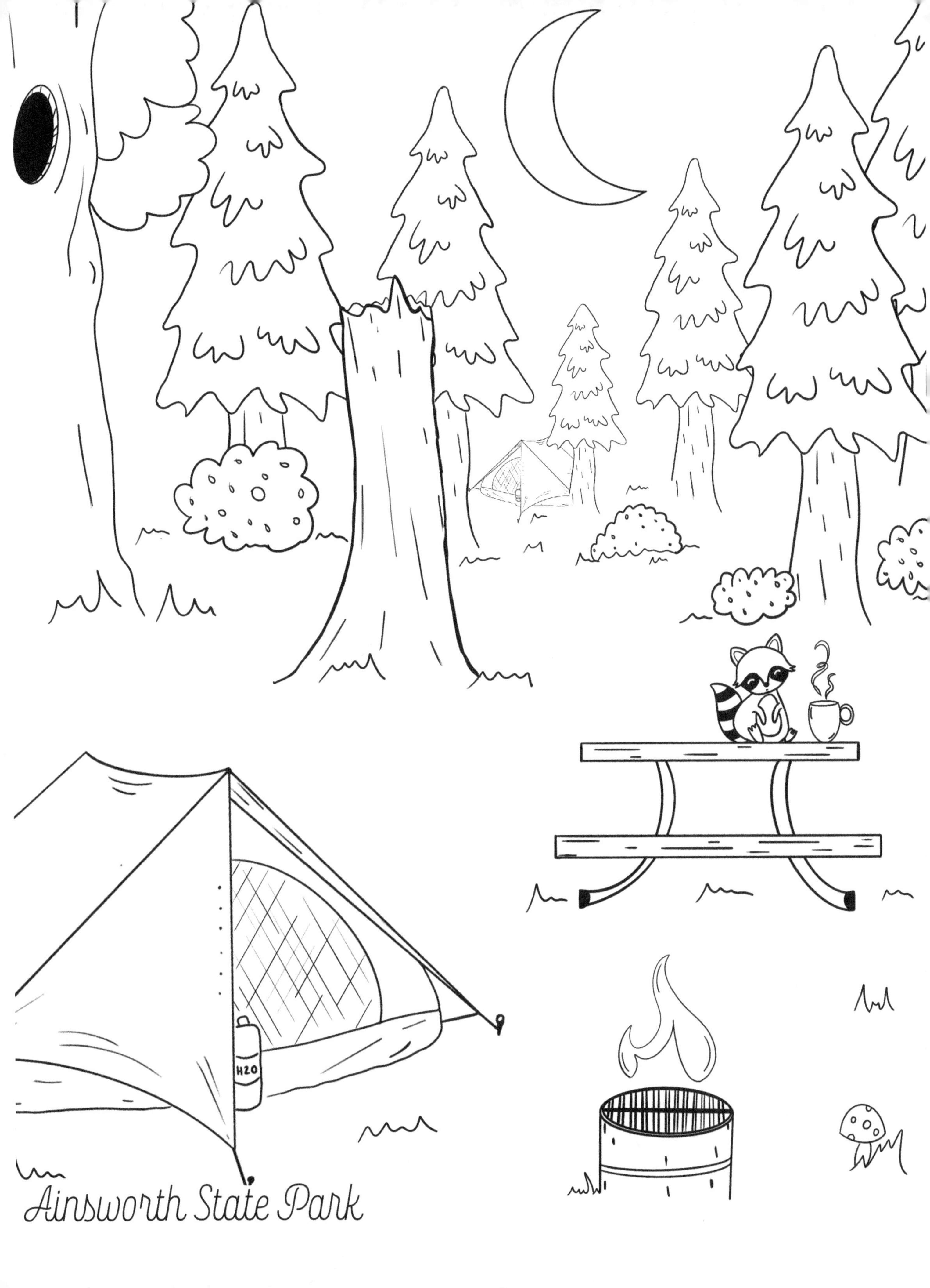

H2O
Ainsworth State Park

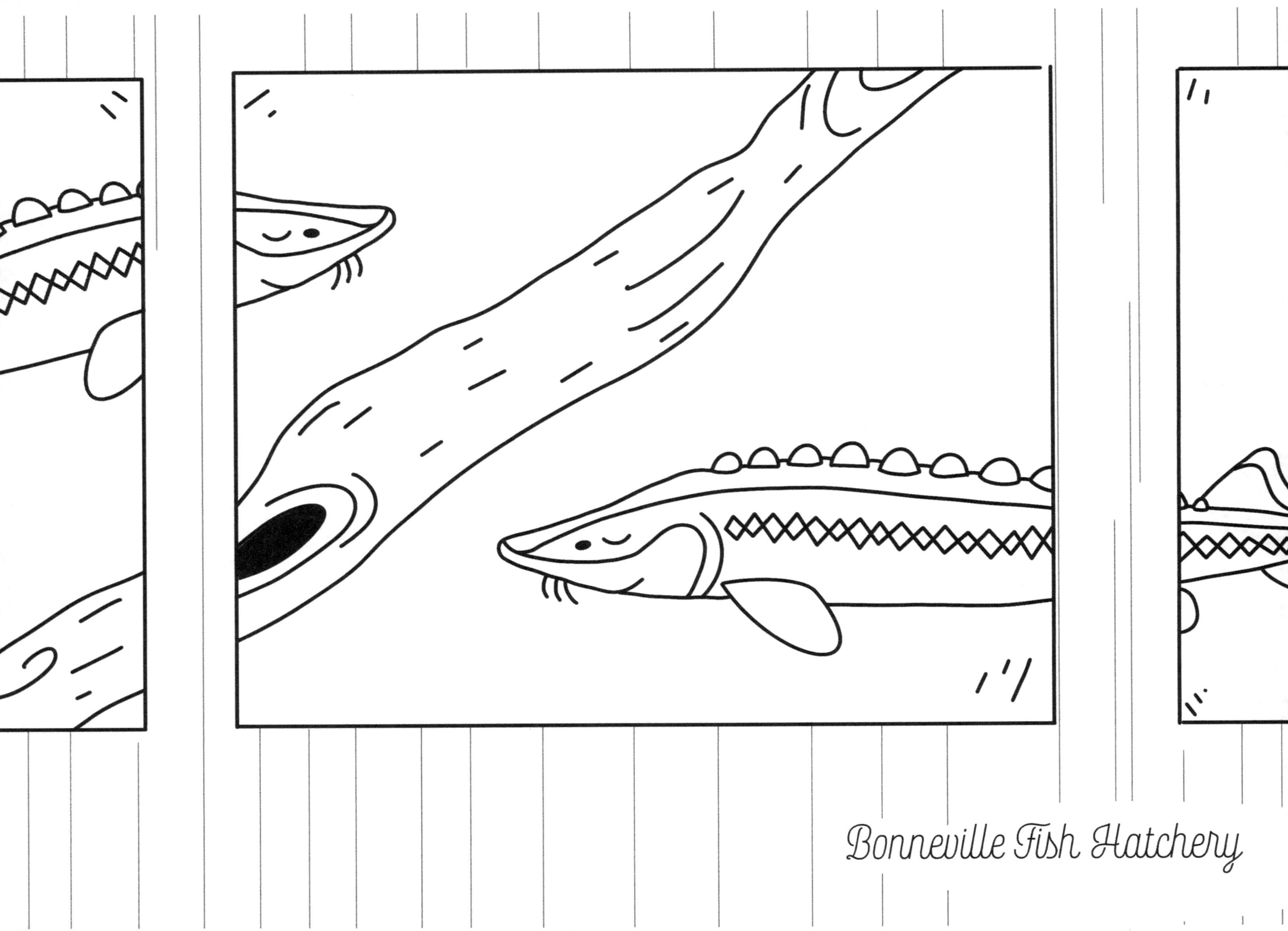

Bonneville Fish Hatchery

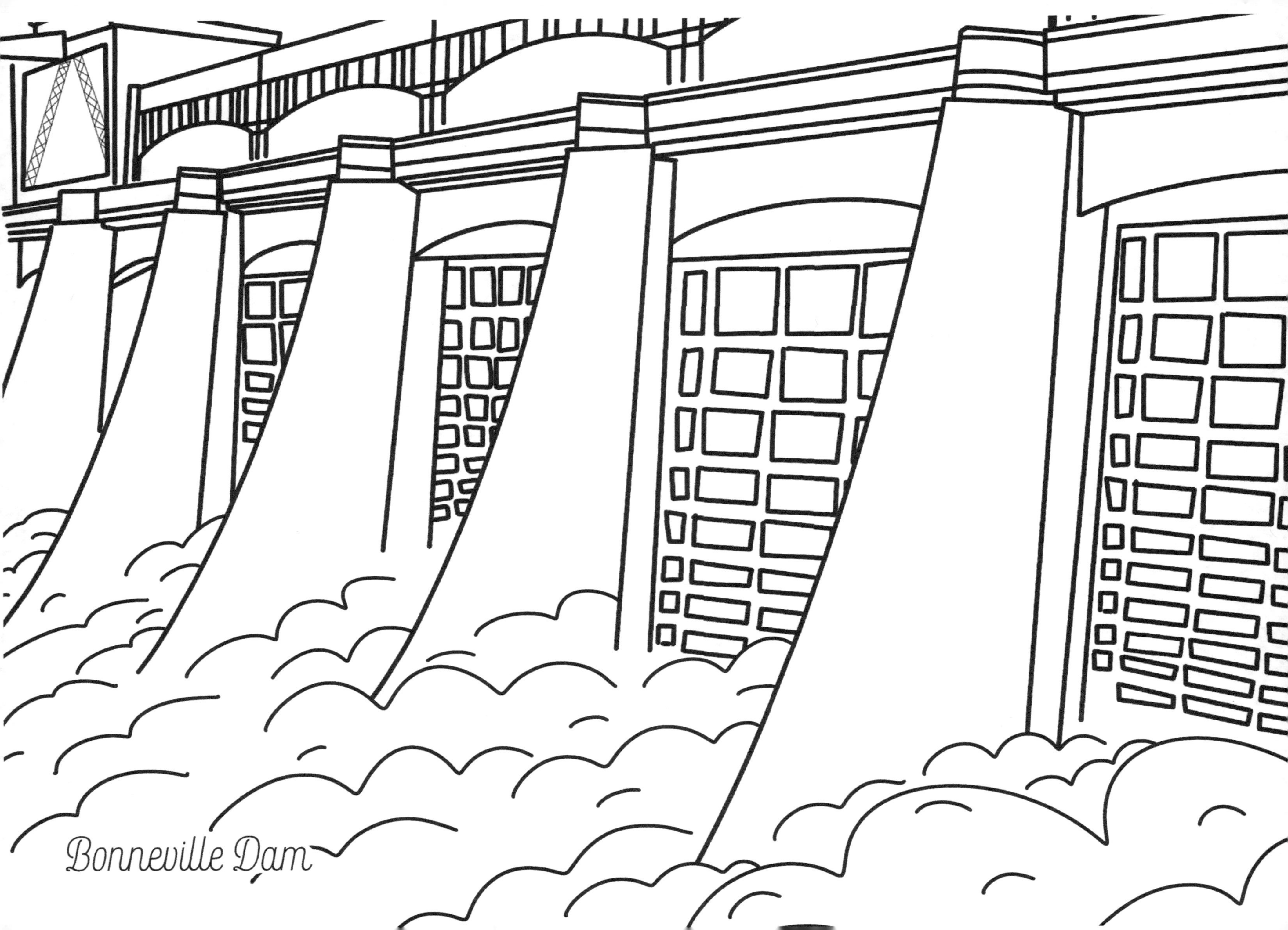

Bonneville Dam

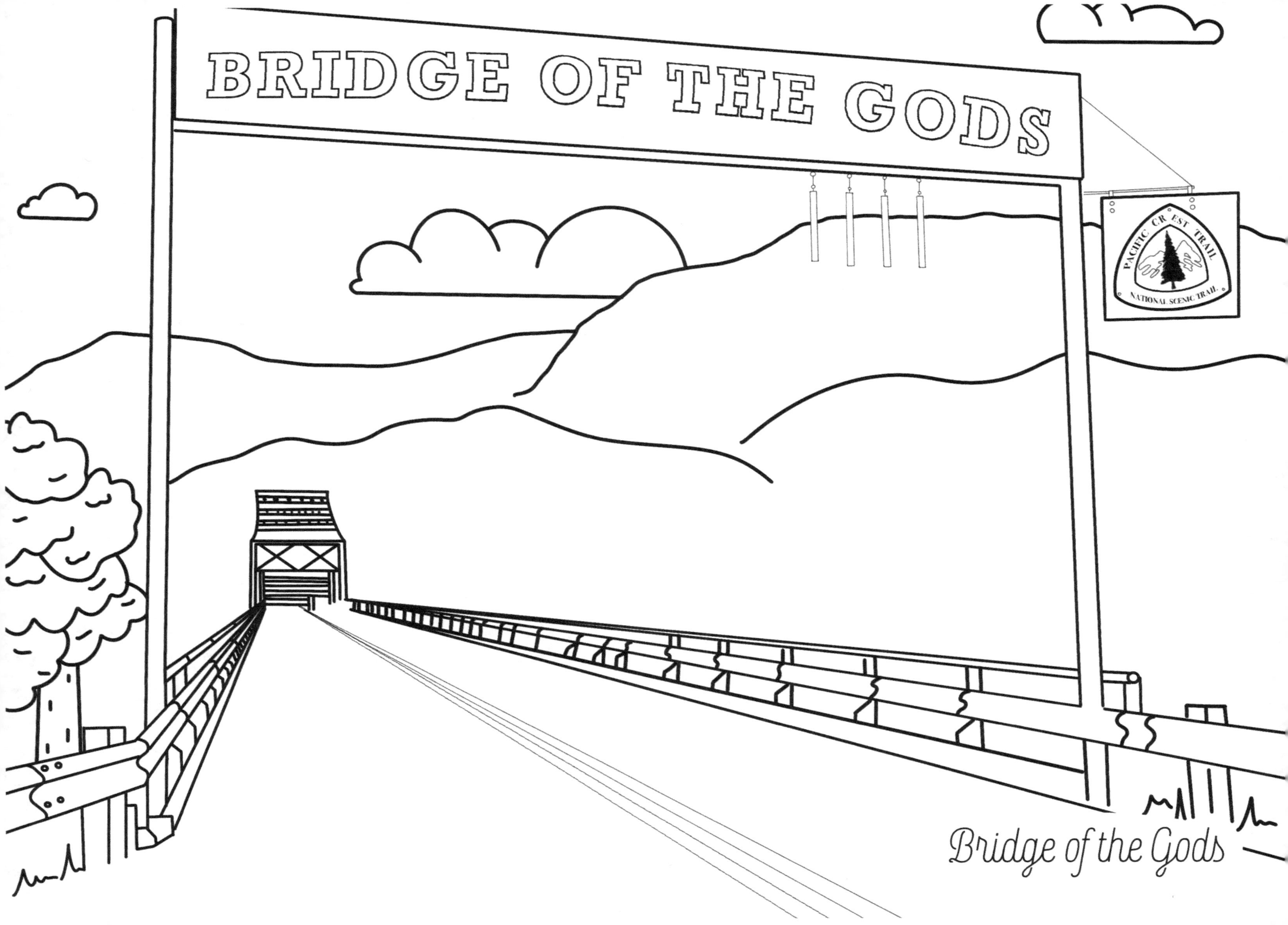

Bridge of the Gods

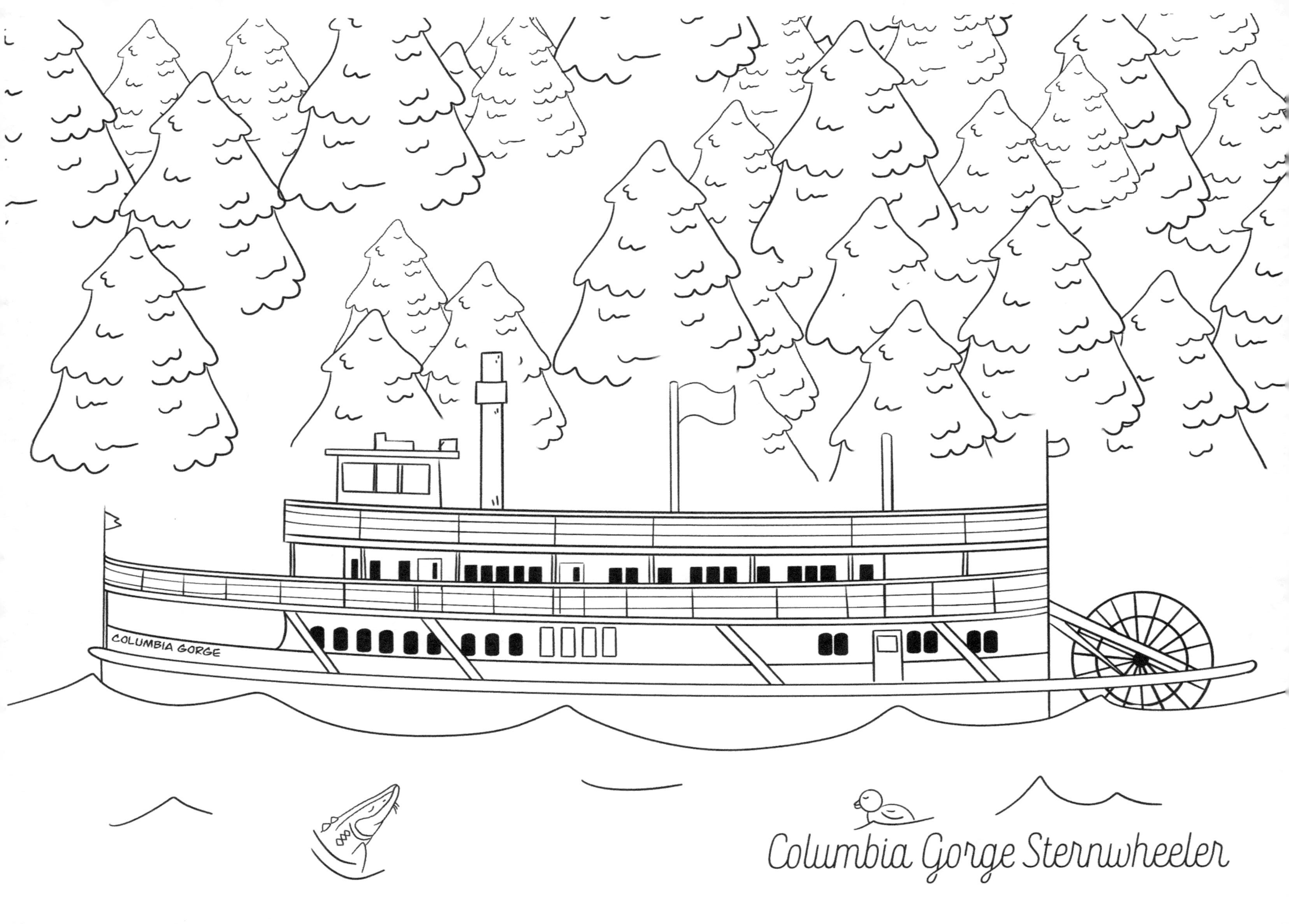

COLUMBIA GORGE
Columbia Gorge Sternwheeler

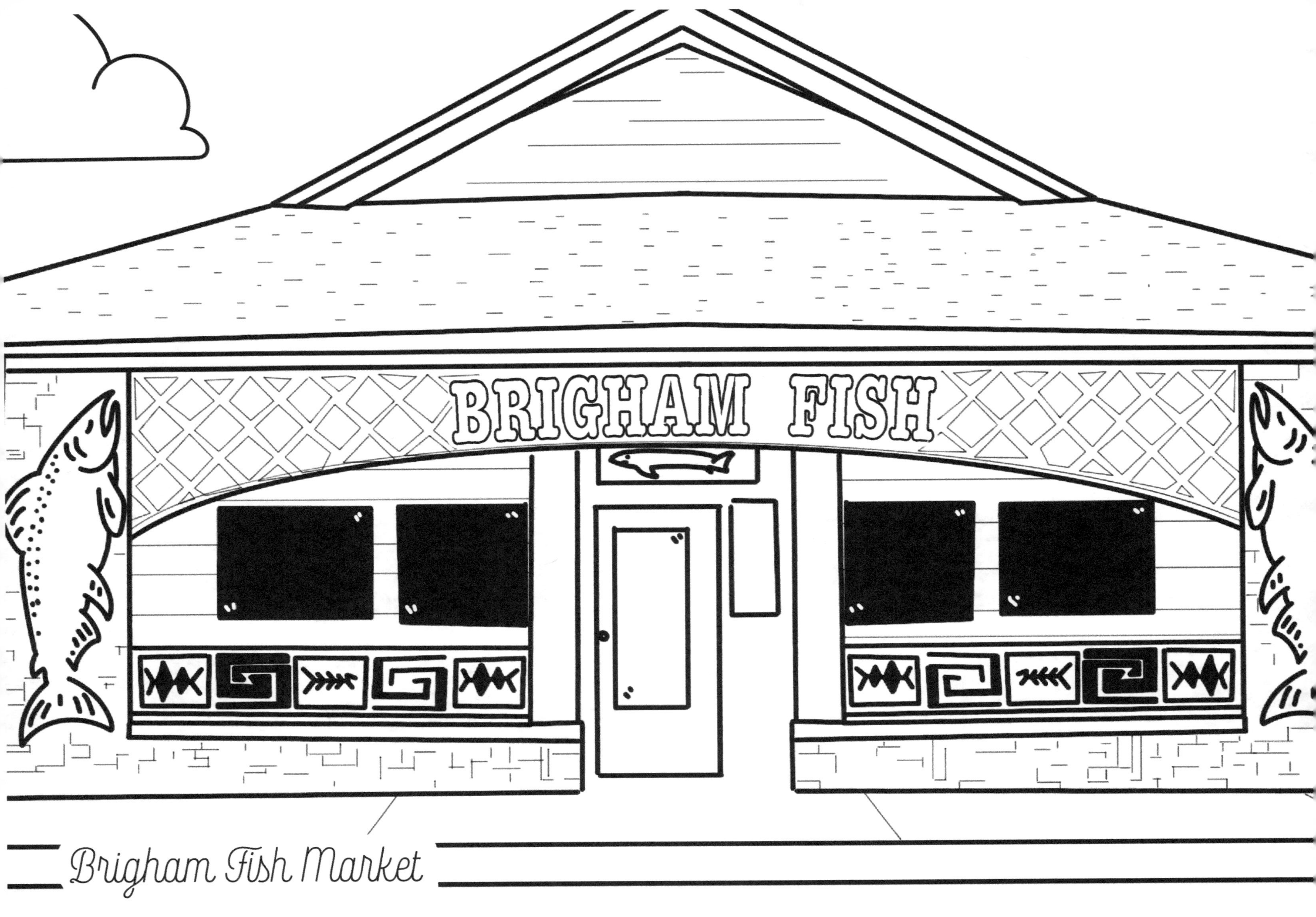

Brigham Fish Market

www.ingramcontent.com/pod-product-compliance
Lightning Source LLC
Chambersburg PA
CBHW080944120726
48003CB00011B/3287